POETIC JOURNEY

Writings on the Water
Poetic Journey:Before, during and after Iraq

NATALIA SERRANO

POETIC JOURNEY:
Writings on the Water

Natalia Serrano
2011/06/27

These poems are a reflection of my journey in life before my decision to join the United States Army, and during my year and a half deployment from 2007 - 2008 OEF/OIF, I had a lot to say what I felt deep down inside, but it was always the mission first and kept my words to myself. However when I returned home from Iraq without thinking I put the pen, pencil and paper away after redeploying ,and just recently decided to let my mind go and allow everyone to share my thoughts, dreams and realities.

9-11-01

My days bright happy to be alive
Good family wonderful wife everything seems all right.
Going to work on that floor
Some other colleagues of mine go to the ground floor.
Getting my cup of coffee at 0715
0830 my world upside down it became
A plane hit,   I was prepared to die,
Rushed to the escape zone, Scrambling to be free
Went down an elevator shaft, god help me
Praying, crying so many people in despair
Must have took an hour or 2
I forgot, out dazed and confused
Looking around for familiar faces
Oh no, another piece of metal hit into the next twin tower
On my hands and knees my wife is there
Save her lord how you saved me.
Tragedy struck and it's to see
How racism, prejudice has destroyed many lives
including mine.
raising three and a widower, I am to be
If I can change back time
I would tell her the many things I wanted to say, endlessly
I must continue life with Joe, Jeremy and little Brittany.

Adore you

You are the one I adore the one I need
God knows you and I, are meant to be
Taught me so much its plain to see
Loving you, you are my destiny
How many times I smiled, and breathe
Babe you're my everything, come to me please.
In my dreams, you are these fantasies,
towards the ceiling, I do stare.
Wondering are you thinking of me
I do of you and one day you will be here
I never want you to go away, closer and near.

Dear Brittany

For you I became who I am
Breaking this welfare chain, Yes I can
Want to be independent, Mommy sure can
I see your beautiful big carefree eyes
Inviting smile little frame
I will never let you down
I am not playing any games
A better life I plan me,
You and whoever is next to me, holding hands
My dreams is to succeed
I am going away for a while, overseas
And when I finish my degree, we will start a newer life
I promise dear daughter Brittany

Falling for you

When we first met, I was incomplete
Searching for the one who can it be
We just met and I just knew
Because out of a million
My eyes found you
Look inside me and see my
Heart is racing endlessly
If ever you decide to come to me
I would give my life's key.

I cried

It's sickening to see the mess, corruption and tragedy
Waking up to this everyday
Wish someone at home could help me pray
Felt lost and no love
Getting a hard attitude
Feeling so cold, alone

Life is hard

I was taught that life was hard
Taking the easy way, better far
Difficult to succeed
Go on in
Life's many dreams turning, Sin
Bumping stones, on roads
Don't go fast, very slow
To achieve life's goals
You are ahead,
looking at the past
Feeling proud for sacrifice
Never family or love that's the recipe
Succeeding in this world, if you're ready come with me
Take my hand, to know reality.

Greatest story

My hero is not so old
She is the greatest story ever told
She looks at me and I am her savior
If she ever knew, I would take her
With me to whatever the place
Now I don't know if I can ever face
They took her from me a DUI
I lay in bed wanted to die
I have some strength left
To get up each and everyday
To look at her tomb at 7 she is already dead
Lord if you heard me
Grant a wish to help others
With this tragedy that every six seconds exist

Withering feathers

Wasn't born in a wealthy family
Silver spoon, yeah not even in dreams
Single mother she strived, making dollars to survive
3 jobs making ends meet, scrubbing floors, waitressing
Catering doing for her children
A better life even delivering newspapers in the morning
light, I admire her for all her sacrifice
This girl named   Sunshine, Lee comfortable living
Father an engineer, mother a credit card freak
Spending so much, ignoring her daughters' fear
Desperation turning to alcohol, prostitution and drugs
was her escape.
Another statistic in this withering life tragedy, a waste.

Tears inside

It's sickening to see the mess, corruption and tragedy

Waking up to this everyday

Wish someone at home could help me pray

Felt lost and no love

Getting hard, tough attitude

Feeling so stone cold, alone

Tears want to fall , I just keep them inside

Better left unsaid like a personal story

In my spirit I did survive

Never meant

I never meant to break your heart
None of the less, destiny broke up apart
Despite it all, I never stopped thinking of you
Dead or alive, where are you tonight, no one ever knew
To me that special someone, I wanted to marry
in the future too.
As time passed by, like the breeze
calling me to that place 13 years to this
anniversary day.

Tears inside

It's sickening to see the mess, corruption and tragedy
Waking up to this everyday
Wish someone at home could help me pray
Felt lost and no love
Getting hard, tough attitude
Feeling so stone cold, alone
Tears want to fall, I just soak them inside
Better left unsaid like a personal story
In my spirit I did survive

From above

Life was over for me , Into 1998
that is what I thought
Into my babe came to me
A blessing from above,
beautiful eyes a smile so sweet, little baby mommy
loves you immensely
I am glad you didn't quit
Fighting at 32 weeks with so much strength, breath and
a mighty fist
Make me so happy
Thank you Lord, for this gift
3 years now and keeps growing
I am proud to be her mom so
Young a youth struggling 2 jobs
Nothing matters it is up to me to get us through.

Mischievously speaking

Do not mistaken this smile on this face
Thoughts in my mind, you can never gravitate
A sly grinning,   that's what you see
Gripping that Adams apple is what I want to do
You can't take me
Who are you kidding, who?
Yes, I am the best   comparing myself to the rest, not in
this lifetime, never that, next

NATALIA   SERRANO

Mind Sweeping

Taller and taller standing shot caller
Marching, starting, going in that pointed direction
To this day no recollection
What did I do, how did I survive
Respond to this request
Forever hold your peace
One day the story would be told,
Wait for it, save
and, behold, PEACE

Life is a reminisce

Beautiful day
Can't complain
Children in school
Up and ready,
Internal song
Symphony within praise
Vroom, zoom, ah Gone!
Living this lifestyle not for everyone to intake
Mission in life, decisions are based
Mine only, never I,
No mistake.
Appreciate beauty, within celebrate
Loving in my soul
Waking up so satisfied, whoa
Never assuming, you are my idol
My wondering fan
When your eyes touch me
It's like a 10th command
Breathing stops and I feel at ease
Warm to the touch
Cold to the hate
My baby despite everything is still holding it down, next
to me.
Until this date.

Description of my Momma

She struggles
So different so strong
Huge responsibility
So much other would break easily
When I am weak, she picks me up
Hugs me tight, Holds me close
And tells me it's gonna be alright, I will see
Sick on some days, as the light never shines
Nevertheless, she is the greatest, her words are never lies
Some may come, others can go
However, momma is there everywhere I grow.

Overwhelmed, Building up

What is wrong with me?
Can't sleep, think, converse or eat
My mind is racing, heart pacing
Darkness overwhelms me, Fear overcomes weak
Deep soul searching, smoking, toking,
At ease, No more joking
Sometimes it feels like my words are choking
Lord I don't take your name in vain keep me focus,
keeping me sane.

Skip beats

Every time I think and it's honestly true

My eyes only see the reflection not a shadow of you

I can't imagine why it can't be

You're the only one that makes my heart skip beats

Babe it's only the truth

Life has been better and my dreams are

finally coming true

Lottery Ultimate Life

If I won lotto how great, it can be
Treated like a golden celebrity
Happy faces, glazed eyes,
Money, money, more more, to entice
Feeling so superficial, Spending my dime
Drinking my champagne, Feeling the lime light
If I won the lottery, Momma would be safe,
Daddy would be free
My brother would stop hanging at the corner;
My sisters would finally listen to me
Life would be less stressed, Working the minimum wage
would cease
I can finally have part of the great American dream.

Nothing is fair

You sit there and have a blank stare
Thinking, wishing, everything were so fair
Nothing in life is an easy fix
Why didn't anybody tell me this script?
I have tried to make it right
Waking up and have realized
It's up to you, make it and survive.

VeRbAL MeSsAgE

I don't know and care if everything is ok
Dark, not smart trying to take it day by day
Breathing, seeing darkness fills me like a haze
You tried to hurt me
Yeah it stung, Trufully
but today its ok, that's yesterday's page
Trying to take my humor, blab la only thing
whispers you say
Those words out your mouth, doesn't faze,
Summertime, it aint cold, choke, who froze
you're lucky you didn't demise,
Who is playing hide and seek, if ever you cross my path,
you will meet
The last thing is my face, might ever see, Take it as is, a
threat, a summons
Mark my words it is the beginnings, Never the end, this
is your verbal warning, do you hear, comprehend.

Protecting the sand

so much to impress

nutting but a terrible, mess reality check

Grappling that gun, trigger spun

Hear this Scared little kid, younger   I seened, don't

have much to give, no one single breath, even to live.

Boy was 8 take anyone down, never hesitate

no words, never choked, point and its all done

9407966R0001

Made in the USA
Charleston, SC
10 September 2011